# Write a Book Quickly

## *Unlock Your Creative Spirit*

## Doug Addison

www.WriteaBookQuickly.com

Write a Book Quickly: Unlock Your Creative Spirit

Copyright © 2011 by Doug Addison

ISBN-13: 978-0-9824618-3-9

ISBN-10: 0-9824618-3-6

Printed in USA by
InLight Connection
PO Box 7049
Santa Maria, CA 93456

Cover design by Cathy Arkle

**For ordering information contact:**

InLight Connection
(800) 507-7853
To order paperback: www.DougAddison.com
To order eBook: www.Writeabookquickly.com

# Table of Contents

## The Treasure Map of Creativity

Creativity can easily get lost in our busy multimedia-stimulated lives. Finding ways to express ourselves is important because it fills a longing we all have to convey more of who we are and why we were created. Ever notice that people want you to know what they value? They have custom "ring-tones" with their favorite song on their cell phones. Some plaster their cars with bumper stickers; others broadcast messages on their t-shirts or ball caps, while many people now have tattoos that tell all. It is part of our need to express who we are and what we value.

Often these small ways of expressing ourselves could be hints about what our true destiny really is. Our life's purpose is like buried treasure within us. We continually receive clues that point to our divinely given gifts and talents. Sadly, very few people discover these gifts and fail to find their greater purpose in life.

If we are not careful, creativity can get stifled and dreams can die. We end up settling for less and get caught in the current of making a living, or in the turbulent waters of past pain and loss. Many people are not even aware that they stay busy to numb the pain of boredom and lack of challenge in their lives. Deep inside we all want to know more about why we are here. We want to contribute to something that is greater than ourselves. We really want to know that our lives on earth could somehow make a difference in the world.

Creativity and expressing ourselves are major door-ways to fulfillment. Igniting passion for who we are and what we like to do will radically change the quality of our lives and the lives of those around us. Creativity is the creation and expression of ideas, thoughts and inspirations. We were all created in God's image and because God is a creator, we all have an integrated desire to create as well. In reality, we are all creative beings with an inherent ability and need to co-create with our creator and one another.

Creativity is often misunderstood. When you tell someone they are creative they often deflect the idea because most people equate creativity with artists, musicians, and designers. Though these are legitimate means of creativity, it actually goes much deeper than this. Creativity can flow through every aspect of life. My desire is to help you ignite passion and find the clues that may be hidden in your life that will help to unlock the doors to creativity and lifelong fulfillment. I want to help you discover your gifts and talents, and to find a life of true fulfillment. It is never too late.

## Lots of Ways to be Creative

There was a time in my life when I played my guitar on a daily basis and I wrote a song at least once a week. Now, I play my guitar much less and seldom write songs. I used to draw and paint and take long walks in nature as a way to stir creativity. Now I write training courses, speeches, and edit audio and video clips on my laptop. I often take very long walks in airports looking for my gate. Though my life has changed, I have discovered my destiny along the way.

I was once much more creative with music, drawing and painting than I am now. For the longest time this frustrated me because I thought I had lost my connection with this area of my life. Somewhere in my mind I thought that for me to be creative I had to write songs, play an instrument, paint, or get in touch with nature. Then I got busy with my career and later, when I would return to one of these other creative outlets, the fulfillment I once had was not as strong as it used to be. I thought my creativity had died and I mourned the loss of a part of my life that was once so expressive.

In relating my experience, I am not trying to downplay these valuable means of creativity. I highly recommend expressing yourself in any way you feel free to do. As I write this, I am in my early fifties and in the midst of a fast-paced lifestyle. Yet, I am learning more about creativity and how to express this life-spring within me.

Several years ago I stumbled upon some gifts and talents that I had no idea existed in me. I discovered some things that I am good at and that gave me an incredible amount of fulfillment. I was surprised to find that my strongest gifts include influencing people through public speaking, writing and making people laugh. Like most people, I dreaded public speaking and I believed that I could not write books because I failed miserably in English class in high school. To this day I have difficulty with spelling and grammar, but I have found ways to work through my weaknesses. Though I have always been naturally funny, I never dreamed that I could actually do stand-up comedy on a stage with professional comedians!

## Finding Your Creative Connection

I had a very small amount of exposure to public speaking. In the 1980s I spoke at a few business training seminars on technology for a company I worked for at the time. I was also given the opportunity occasionally to teach a class at my church. At first I tried to be like other speakers with perfect notes, quotes and clear points. One day a friend and mentor of mine encouraged me to "just be me" when I spoke publicly. He told me that if I would simply let my passion for the subject come out, be spontaneously funny and learn to connect with my audience, I would someday be a very successful speaker.

At first I did not understand what he was saying, but I took his advice and began to practice. I was amazed at the response that I got from people. I found that I have a knack for making things simple, understandable and practical. When I spoke this way, it gave people hope that they can do it too. I crossed over from training people with theory, facts, and head-knowledge to imparting life-giving insight and stories that created new hope in people. I began to experience a deep level of personal fulfillment through writing and public speaking because I had found a way to contribute to making the world a better place by restoring hope and life to people.

It was not just my speaking style or the words I chose that made me a successful public speaker, although that helped. I felt as though God's Creative Spirit was flowing through me as I spoke. I seemed to know what each crowd needed and I tailored my talks to make the most impact. I noticed that when I went back to speaking from notes and points, there was not as much impact at all. In fact, those were often the most disastrous talks I have ever done.

I surmised from this that being creative is a key that allows words to be transformed to Spirit. And it is the Spirit that transforms lives. Wow, was that a deep realization. As a public speaker, most of the training I received was on how to study, write and present material. But I had not been told that if I actually "lived" what I was talking about and got passionate about it, and if I could find ways to be funny and down to earth, then God would actually turn words into life.

Now I speak in front of tens of thousands of people each year. I make people laugh and help awaken them to the possibilities of transforming their lives and empower them to be all that they were created to be. I mix my talks with stand-up comedy routines, real life stories, practical exercises and "surprisingly applicable" music. I am convinced that music has a major impact on people. So in the middle of a talk I play songs such as "Don't Worry Be Happy" and "I Can See Clearly Now."

Unfortunately, I did not discover my speaking, writing, and comedy gifts until I was over forty years old. I have determined that this does not need to be the case for everyone. That is why I am committed to helping people find their purpose in life as early as possible. I meet so many people who are living their lives with unclear or clouded vision. Many are people who are disconnected from their true passions and God-given gifts and talents. *Imagine the possibilities if people everywhere began to discover their talents, gifts and ultimately their life's purpose. Yes, the world would be a much better place.*

## Discovering Clues About Ourselves

Looking back on my process I can see that I never really fit in well with traditional training and education. I am not trying to be disrespectful to teachers and educators. However, within a short period of time in almost any class or training I took, I would usually find faster and more efficient ways of doing things. Before I knew this about myself, I often experienced conflict and even hostility with my co-workers and peers. They thought I was out to get their jobs when in reality I was trying to help create a harmonious environment for everyone to operate at their highest potential and for the organization to become more efficient and profitable.

Because most people did not recognize my "out-of the-box" talents, I spent a number of years feeling frustrated and unsure about where to turn to develop my skills. After reflecting on my life, I can pinpoint a few key individuals who made the most impact on my life, namely: my sixth-grade teacher, my high school Distributive Education teacher, a pastor, and a business/ministry leader. They went out of their way to help me. They spoke positively to me and allowed me to be myself. They all encouraged me to go beyond my comfort zone and took me places with them and allowed me to write and speak. They were the ones who recognized my talents and though I did not see it for the longest time, I actually spent most of my life feeling that there was something wrong with me because I did not fit in.

Interestingly, I did not do well at all in high school speech, art, and writing classes. Now I can clearly see how my gifts began to emerge, although I did not know it at the time. I guess I should have seen the clues when I did things like practical training, persuading people, and making people laugh. When I did these things I was the most successful. Unfortunately I was extremely shy, had low self-esteem and was quiet most of my life, which caused me to withdraw and play my guitar mostly by myself.

Here are a few clues that, as I look back in my life, were there all along, pointing me towards speaking, writing and comedy.

Clue #1 "Have it Your Way." In my high school speech class, I was not good at public speaking at all. As a matter of a fact, I equated giving a speech with a near-death experience, next to riding on a rollercoaster or getting a root canal. Then I did a demonstration speech on "How to Make a Whopper®." I had worked at Burger King for several years as a teenager and had been promoted to shift leader. I brought in all the fixin's and wore my red paper hat. I dressed the part and made everyone laugh. I made jokes about being the best "Whopper® flopper" which was a term I coined for wrapping the big burger fast. I had a great time in front of people and I got an A when "I did it my way." It was one of the first times that I felt comfortable speaking in front of people. What I did not realize until later is that I am a natural at practically instructing people.

Clue #2 "Did you know you are a good speaker?" After barely graduating from high school and dropping out of college, I worked as a manager in banking, finance and administration. During the 1980s the "cross-training" concept was becoming popular. In several of the companies where I worked in California, they required every manager to develop a training course educating other departments about what we did. The concept was to develop a bigger picture for everyone so they could see how their jobs impacted the entire company. As a young up-and-coming manager, I found that when I spoke in front of groups in the corporate environment for training purposes, I got a lot of positive feedback and was often invited to address the annual sales meeting and to emcee Christmas parties.

Clue #3 "Did anyone ever tell you that you are funny?" All my life people have told me that I am funny. I was the youngest of four in my family and I was the cut-up who loved to make everyone laugh. Sometimes it was just to help lighten the environment of growing up in a troubled but loving family. The strange thing is: I am terrible at remembering and telling jokes. If I ever made people laugh it was all "off the cuff" and I could not remember what I said afterwards. Later I found out that this is actually called improvisation (or "Improv") and that there are many improvisational comedians in the world that can make real-life stories funny.

Clue #4 "Hey did you know you are a good writer?" I once worked for an organization that started a magazine on spirituality. We were told that employees could submit articles but we would be going up against professional writers for consideration to be published. My first article got rejected several times before getting published. The editor commented to me that with a little practice I could be a very good writer. Wow, even though I never had thought about being a writer, today I have published dozens of articles, as well as several books and training manuals.

All these clues pieced together like a treasure map that eventually guided me to my ultimate purpose in life: to help millions of people transform their lives while I have fun, laugh, and grow in all that I do.

## Personal Application

1. Looking at your life, who are people that have impacted or influenced you the most?

2. Thinking about your life, what are three or four ways that you have enjoyed expressing yourself?

3. What things do you do regularly to be creative? (e.g., journal, blog, paint, garden, scrapbook, take photos, decorate, cook, do woodworking, develop websites, etc.)

4. Are there any clues in your life that may be pointing to things that you are passionate about?

5. If you knew you could not fail and money was no object, name at least three things that you would like to do.

**Notes**

## Writing is Art Too!

As I mentioned previously, early in my life I was a musician and I wrote poetry and lyrics at least once a week. This slowly faded as I got a corporate job and had a family. After I thought my ability and passion to write had died, suddenly it was as if this gift was rebirthed in me. After having a successful twenty-year career in business I decided to "cash out" at age forty and go for things I have always wanted to do. I have always known that my ultimate destiny was in to help people. For me, "life is ministry," so the idea of going into ministry seemed unnatural.

My wife and I felt directed by God to start a new kind of church that would cater to people who don't like church. So I became a new type of pastor of a very unusual type of church in a Midwest college town. I left my corporate job to fulfill my life destiny of changing the world one person at a time. I discovered rather quickly that I was able to impact people through my gift of communication. At first I was not all that good at writing sermons but I had a knack for getting a point across. When I first started developing sermons or "influential talks" as I liked to call them, it would take me over twelve hours to develop a thirty-five minute talk. This included research, writing, editing, and practicing my delivery before I delivered the message so to speak. I tell people to not put me in a box because I am not like any Christian you have ever met before!

I have to admit that from a speaking standpoint, being the pastor of a church was not an easy job. You have to develop spiritually encouraging messages 52 weeks a year and deliver them to many of the same people. To be honest with you, I often resorted to copying ideas from other sermons, audios, and books I read. This is common practice among pastors and there is nothing wrong with it. Later I became a conference speaker and I quickly found that oftentimes the author of a book I used to develop a message was sitting on the front row looking at me! This was all the more reason for me to learn to write and develop my own material.

I remember one day when I was feeling discouraged about writing and speaking. A mentor told me, "Don't forget what you already know. Just be yourself. You know how to do this, just do what you do best again and again and eventually it will work for you." The key is to major on your strengths and practice a lot.

After writing and delivering thousands of speeches, sermons, and training talks, God began to direct me to focus on a particular message that is needed in the world today. I have always wanted to help people find their destiny in God. I call it the lost art of love and encouragement. I was soon invited to speak at all types of events to a variety of different audiences.

## Finding Your Life Message

As a speaker or writer we all have a message or topic we are passionate about. This is our life message. You'll notice that the more you speak or write, the more you will begin to default to a particular theme. It may take time to formulate the actual message but you are most likely rehearsing it right now. It is the topic that you tend to mention or refer to during your conversations, speeches, and writing. Usually a life message is something that we have experienced or have conquered in our lives. It could be things like overcoming emotional wounds, family values, political convictions, or a hobby or sport that we love to do. A life message is important to discover because anything that you have passion for will bring you the most satisfaction. People can detect writers and speakers who are teaching based on theory as opposed to life experience or passion.

For me, I realized that I was drawn to helping people in need. No matter what I talked or wrote about I was always slipping something in about it. Although my life message has morphed over the years, it is still laid on the foundation of loving people. Begin to notice what themes or topics you are drawn to most. As you study and write on it more, you will begin to see a life message emerge. Having a life message does not mean that this is the only subject or topic you will write about. You will find that the passion for your life message will flow into all of your other writing. Another passion I have is public speaking. So I am writing this book from a speaker and writer's perspective.

## Ways To Start Writing

Over time I began to formulate a message that I presented when I went to speak at seminars, conferences, and churches. I knew that God was directing me to write a book and people really liked my message, but I did not have any practical experience as a writer. To help develop myself in this area and gain practical experience, I started with writing blogs and magazine articles. Without knowing whether they would ever be published, I created a portfolio of articles to show I was serious. I started by posting them on websites. Now people write all the time and use Internet blogs as their means of publication. There are lots of websites on the Internet designed specifically to allow you to post articles. I will list a few later in this book.

Most of my early articles were turned down, but I got a few published in a small local newspaper and two magazines. Let me give you some great insight. I quickly found that most magazine articles should be 1200 words or less. The first one I wrote was well over 1800 words and it was quickly rejected. Later I realized that the articles I wrote and posted on my website that were between 800 and 1200 words long were often picked up for publication on other websites and in magazines. The longer articles were not. In fact, 500–600 word articles work best for blogs.

To learn to write shorter, more concise articles I started doing writing exercises. I took my longer 1800+ word articles and rewrote them until they were 1200, 1000, 800, 500, and even 300 words. At first I thought it would be impossible to get it down to 300 words, but I did. One of my 300 word articles that was originally over 1000 words got published as a "sidebar" in a magazine on dreams. Once I learned the discipline of writing shorter pieces that could make a clear point with fewer words, I found that more of them were published. Less is definitely more if you want to hold someone's attention. Learn to get to the point as quickly as possible. People who read articles are often too busy to read books.

## How I Wrote a Book Quickly

In 2002, I was awakened at five o'clock in the morning with the urge to "get up and write." I got up and was inspired to write in the early hours of the morning before work over the next two weeks. During this inspired time I wrote a small outline for what I hoped to be someday be a book. Then I spent the next two years avoiding finishing the rest of the manuscript. I had a lot of good reasons. First, I am not a writer. From there, my list of excuses progressed even more: I don't have time to write, what if people don't like it, what if I fail in front of the whole, entire world, etc.

My problem was I was trying to be too perfect. I was comparing myself to other writers and forgot about the lesson I had learned years earlier about public speaking, "If I am myself then things will flow."

Here's what I discovered about myself. I knew I had a destiny to write a book and I even had the start of an outline. I was a successful conference speaker and my schedule was filled a year in advance. I took the outline I had written and developed a training workshop that was helping thousands of people all around the world. I had done all the research for the new book idea and even road-tested my ideas by doing live events for several years so I knew that it worked. People everywhere were telling me they wanted to read my book once I wrote it.

So what was stopping me? Though I was not con- sciously aware of it, I came to realize that I had fear of failure. It was so painful every time I sat down to write, because I had never written a book before, and as I mentioned previously, I was never that good at English class in school. I had thoughts of the book turning out really bad and people not liking it. I also had to submit it to a publisher and it was going to be read by many of my colleagues and highly respected friends.

However, what if I did not write it and later in life I realized that I missed a great opportunity? What if someone else wrote a book similar to mine and it was successful? On the other hand, what if I did write it? Possibly tens of thousands of people all over the world could read it and be changed. I would begin to generate revenue from the sales that would allow me to do more events and impact even more people. The fact was: I would experience much more gain by writing it than not writing it. I had to come to a place where I realized that *not* writing my book was actually more painful than the pain of writing it.

Okay, now I was convinced. However, writing it was still very hard for me. I needed to find a way to make this painful process enjoyable and fun. Even though I do not drink much coffee, I really love going to places like Starbucks® and hanging out at coffee houses where I feel really inspired. So I went to Starbucks® every day, and within three weeks I had written the initial manuscript. I have to admit my rear was a bit sore from those wooden chairs, but I found a way to make writing fun. I listened to music during the process and got to know other people who were there writing too.

As it turned out, my first book was liked by thousands of people, and I am so glad I broke through and found a way to get myself to write it. Now I love to write, and it is not a painful process at all. Since then, I write almost on a daily basis. My fear was holding me back from a gift that I didn't even know I had.

I have gotten dozens of emails from people who have heard me talk about this and have successfully written their own books in a matter of weeks. If you want to break through and accomplish the things you want in life, you must follow through and find out what it is that is stopping you. So let's take a look at what might be holding you back.

## Jump-Start Yourself

Here's an exercise that will change your life forever. Most of us have a lifestyle of putting things off. I have discovered secrets for what I call a "Breakthrough Lifestyle." It is learning to do small things consistently towards what we want to accomplish. Over time your small steps will build up to huge accomplishments and it will not take you a lot of effort because you will do them in bite-size tasks. You can read more about this in my book *Personal Development God's Way.*

## Exercise: What are you putting off?

One of the most difficult things about changing your life is simply getting started. Once you take the first step, you start to see how easy it is, you develop momentum, and eventually it will become a new good habit. Making a decision to act is what will change your life. You will move from just believing it is a good thing—to actually doing it. This is what separates those who obtain what they want from the ones who just talk about it.

This exercise does not have to be about writing. I am going to ask you to find something in your life that you are putting off. This is something that if you were to do it, your life would change in some way. It does not have to be anything major.

## 1. Make a decision

What are a few decisions or tasks you have been putting off? Remember, these are things that would change your life in some way. Maybe you want to take steps to get out of debt, lose weight, reconcile a broken relationship, clean up your office, write a book, go to college, or take a vacation? Write a few of them down.

## 2. Do something

Now choose one of the things you wrote and think of one or two simple steps you can do today that will help you with your new decision. These are simple, baby steps. Do you need to write a letter or email to someone? Make a phone call? Purchase a book, DVD, or organizer? Make sure you are specific and follow through by doing it now or today.

## 3. Be consistent

Now commit to doing this exercise every week. Look for one or two things that you would like to accomplish by the end of the week and write them down. Then come up with a practical step you can take and do it. As this becomes a habit you will eventually have a lifestyle of breaking through instead of avoidance.

## Writing Tips I Learned the Hard Way

I am going to get really practical for a moment. Here are some tips and tricks I wish someone would have told me when I was starting out. They can benefit you even if you are an experienced writer.

- I gave up the idea that I would write perfectly the first time through. I began by simply writing as if I was talking to a close friend or telling a group my story. I did not worry about grammar and structure—I found that editors help fix all that later. As the writer/creator, learn to just sit down and let it flow.

- Write to an audience of one. The more personal and down to earth you can sound the more people will like your writing. I mentioned writing as if you are talking to a friend. I found that I had to convey this to my publisher ahead of time and asked them to be careful to not use flowery language, big words, and impressive statements.

- I started by writing a summary of what I wanted my book to be about, who the target audience was, and a page or so of just a bunch of thoughts about what I wanted to say. This helped me to keep a clear focus on whom I was speaking to and what I was trying to communicate.

- I created a simple outline to start. Then I began to write freely under each outline heading. At first I was discouraged because of the size of the document. I wondered how it would ever become a book. Listen to me; trust the process and it will fill up as you go. You can go back later and insert more details, research, stories, and revisions later on.

- Maybe you are more disciplined than I am, but I found that as I was writing a non-fiction book, I had a lot of opinions and rants that kept seeping into my writing. The last thing a person wants to read is your pet peeve. People are looking for solutions, not reaffirmations of what is wrong. So I made a habit of writing a "rant page" before I worked on my project. I dumped all my aggression and disappointments into a one-page document that I would set aside and then start clean with a better attitude. I often had to do this several times during my writing process. This allows you to sound positive and get to the point with solutions.

As I continued to work on the outline, it began to develop into chapter headings. Then I went back through and read what I wrote and made corrections and wrote more. After every completion I would go back through my work adding more and more, allowing it to evolve organically. It is similar to creating a tapestry, needlepoint or knitting. Each pass will bring more clarity.

- I rearranged things quite a bit in the process and kept track of what I wanted to add and things I removed. A good habit is to create a new folder on your computer to put your old documents in every time you make any major changes. Be sure to save older versions and make backups of your documents. As the chapters developed I created three or four bullet points at the top for each chapter of what I was trying to say and who I was saying it to—this kept me focused on the point that I wanted to get across and minimized rabbit trails.

- Because my book was non-fiction, I went through it again and added stories, quotes and research. It was like a play or a musical that unfolded over time. I went back over it adding more and more, allowing it to develop.

- My second book was quite different. I had first developed it as a training course. So when I went back to convert it to a manuscript two years later, I had to add and move chunks of text. I found it helpful to print out the entire book and tape each chapter to the walls of my office (a.k.a. the dining room at the time). Since I am visual I could see things that needed to be moved and I could literally cut the pages and move them on the wall then go back and make the adjustments on my computer.

## Practical Tips for Writing a Manuscript

- Be careful about whom you share it with. I have heard too many stories of people who share their writing with trusted friends and family members who give discouraging feedback. Sometimes it is best to find a person who has experience in analyzing written documents. People who do it for a living are able to see your diamonds that might be a little rough for others to recognize. They are also better at encouraging you. Make sure they are encouraging before you share your work.

Most manuscripts are required to be submitted in the *Chicago Manual of Style* format. Unless you understand how to do this, it is best to have a professionally trained editor and proofreader do it for you. Just don't let it stop you. I have heard of people submitting very raw documents and publishers accepting them in any condition if they like the subject or material. I submitted my first manuscript in a Microsoft Word document "double spaced" and it went through to publishing just fine. Now Microsoft Word has "style formats" for a manuscript that will do it all for you. Just highlight the entire document and choose the manuscript style. You can always hire a professional proofreader or formatting specialist by using a website like www.elance.com.

- Always keep your eye out for ideas to add to your writing project. Do the research as you go. I try to keep three separate folders for each writing project, and you may find this works for you as well: keep one in your email program that you can copy related emails or website links to, another word processing folder with subfolders to organize your work and track things to add, what you deleted, quotes, research statistics etc., and the third is a paper folder to keep magazine articles or any printed material you get over time. This system will allow you to capture material whenever you come across it.

- Get creative in how you capture your ideas. You can use your cell phone or digital camera when you see something that relates to your book; just take a picture and email or copy it to your computer. I have a large dry erase board next to my desk. I am constantly writing outlines and ideas and taking a digital picture and filing it in my computer folder for that particular book.

- When writing on a word processor, be sure to utilize the Track Changes feature when sending your document to be edited by someone else. (Not all programs have this feature. Be sure to check before you begin.) Always keep several versions of your writing. I create an entirely new file each time I do major changes, that way I can go back and restore things I took out if needed. If you are technically oriented then you may want to become familiar with your word processing program. Just don't let it sidetrack you. If you are not a geek, (i.e., tech-oriented) then don't worry about it, just write. At a minimum you can learn some keyboard shortcuts for repeated tasks.

- Caution—if you use any quotes from other books, you are usually required to get the author or publisher's permission to use the quote yourself. There are services that will get permission for many popular published quotes for you. Be sure to save all your permissions in a secure location. I use a simple spreadsheet to track the exact details of the quotation, where I got it, how they want to be credited, etc. I also check off each quote in the spreadsheet as I get the permission.

- Always make a backup copy of your work. Back up your computer files to an external source and make several different backups and store them in different places (in case of fire or theft). If I have recently written a lot and I don't have time to do a backup, I just email it to myself or to a friend. You can create a free email account on services like Google or Hot Mail for this purpose. If you have hand-written journals or notes, invest in an inexpensive fireproof safe. A friend of mine had a dream that her house caught fire so she bought a fireproof safe for her writing journals. Ten years later her house burned to the ground and her precious journals were all safe.

- Consider doing long-term backups of your files. You can burn your writing folder on a CD or copy it to a USB drive and keep it in a secure location different than your house or office. I can't say enough about backups!

## Just Write, Be Yourself and Find Your Style

Whether you are writing fiction, non-fiction, screenplays, training manuals, sermons, comedy, or whatever, it is so important that you find a style of writing that suits you. When you are yourself, you will feel more natural. There are millions of published books but only a few seem to draw the attention of people. Although it would be nice to do, you don't have to write a bestseller. I like to compare writing to singing a song. Sometimes you sing just for the sake of singing for yourself or audiences of various sizes. Sometimes you will write just for the sake of writing. It does not have to be published in order to be valuable. I write nearly every day but not everything I write ever makes it into a published form. That is why I keep a computer journal. It allows me to write thoughts and ideas and then cross-reference and search for them later.

Some people have a strong ability to write touching emails. They can pour out empathy to others and impart compassion through their words. Unfortunately, most people with this unique ability do not realize they have a creative writing gift. We often put creativity in a box. If people open up with you and share their problems on a regular basis then there is a good chance that you have a strong creative listening and compassion gift. I am finding that many people who are good listeners are also good at expressing themselves and are potentially good writers with the right coaching.

## My Discovery About Writing

When my wife Linda and I were on our honeymoon we went to a small island in the Canadian Puget Sound. The place where we stayed was a writing retreat house for several world famous theologians and authors. At that time I did not have any writing experience and frankly did not realize that I was destined to write. The retreat house had bookshelves lined with hundreds of classics from the past hundred years.

Early in the morning while looking out the window adoring God's beautiful nature, I felt inspired to write. For the next four hours I wrote with great passion, gaining spiritual insight from God's Spirit and books that I felt drawn to. I was stunned at what I had created. Then as suddenly as the inspiration had hit me, my computer froze up (it was a Mac in case you are wondering) and I lost the document completely. I could not remember what I had written and was never able to recreate it. My loving new wife said that I should think of it as a song that was sung and not meant to be recorded. That helped me gain perspective that not all writing is for the purpose of publication. What I wrote was placed in my spirit and would be available later. I had not yet read my chapter on saving and making backups of your writing.

A few years later I began writing instructional technical documents for the company I worked for. I also wrote several practical training seminars for my church. It was then that I realized that my style is not like most typical writers. I am a practical "how-to" guy.

Early on I did not have an outlet for my writing. This was long before the invention of the Internet blog in which anyone can post their writings for others to read. I purchased a web domain name and developed a website in the 1990s called dougaddison.com. Over the years it has been the outlet for my articles, comedy, practical instruction, and now my speaking seminars as well.

## Writing Your Blog or Your Manuscript

Internet blogs are a great way to start writing or be an outlet to keep your creative juices flowing. Most people who use the Internet do so for two major reasons, entertainment and information. Blogs and articles provide exactly these two things. The more you can keep the balance, the more interesting it is for a reader. If you have no previous experience in online work, you might wonder how the readers can help you earn money when it is free to read content. The catch here is 'marketing'. It is important to market your work out there, regardless of whether you want to sell a cookbook or a book on the best blogging tips in the world.

That doesn't imply that you need to sell someone's product or commercialize your article or blog. Although that is an option, most writers, in its true sense, don't really like the idea of commercializing their blogs. There are countless online writers who write completely personal or non-commercial blogs and still manage to earn a good amount of money. The key is a term called "monetizing." If you are able to provide your audience with something fresh and unique, chances are that they will love it, and will talk to others about it. This will promote your content further. People will pay for information if it is presented well.

You can create your own personal blog and write about whatever you want. My advice is to avoid doing what most people do—that is, they fill their blogs with what they had for breakfast and reasons why they are not blogging. If you are going to take the time to blog, at least come up with something of interest. It is amazing how many people from all over the world will read your blog if it is appealing to their situation. Remember that whatever you post on the Internet never goes away. Be selective on how personal you want to be.

You can create a specialty or niche blog about recipes, diets, survival techniques, surfing, or whatever interests you. Unlike the old days of sending out spam emails to promote your blog or book, you can attract people through the Internet to visit your blog through search engine optimization (SEO). This is done by placing "keywords" in your blog or article so that people with an interest in that subject can find you through an Internet search. Once they visit, it is possible to run small non-invasive ads on your blog called Affiliate Partnerships. You can write a review on a book and insert a link to buy it on Amazon. If someone goes to your website or blog and clicks to buy something in an ad that you recommend, then you get a percentage of the sale. This is a great new way to make residual income while increasing the traffic to your website or blog. It can be done tastefully and people are used to seeing ads on blogs that relate to the article or content they are reading. If you are an expert in an area then people want to know what you recommend. People are looking and willing to pay for fast information.

An example of this is that I have extensive training in dream interpretation. So my website draws people through the Internet who have this interest. I have a small ad for a computer dream journal that I use myself and highly recommend to others. For every purchase of the software through my website, my organization gets a percentage of the sale. My intent is not to make money, but to help people. I have been using this computer journal for years and love it so I created a series of free training videos on how I use it for writing and as a dream journal. It is my way of helping people to get the most out of their writing experience. I recommend using only products that you believe in and know would benefit others.

Here's some amazing news that most people are not aware of. If you are naturally gifted with good writing abilities and you know how to use the Internet then you have the opportunity to earn amazing amounts of income through the Internet. The Internet has become the new money making tool of our generation that allows you to earn money at home. We are at the beginning of a new wave in which people can make a lot of money through their online businesses. The number of online writers making a decent income is also astounding. It is not always easy and there are certain trials and tribulations any author has to go through in order to reach the pinnacle of success. It is not a "get rich quick" opportunity and it usually takes time to build an online reputation. I have a chapter on marketing your books using social-media and blogging later in this book.

## More Writing Tips

I wrote this book over a period of three years. It started with someone asking me how I wrote my first book. Several years ago I wrote a half page of practical instructions on how I wrote my first manuscript. I would email it to people I met who expressed a sincere interest in writing and looked like they needed help. I kept adding to the document until it finally evolved into the book you are reading right now.

I travel a lot and speak at seminars and conferences around the world. I have very little time alone in quiet places where I can feel creative. Most of the writing I have done in this book has been on airplanes, sitting in airports, or in busy coffee shops, like the one I'm in right now as I write this chapter (I am sitting in a Starbucks® Coffee shop in Seattle, Washington).

I do realize that not everyone has the same type of personality or lifestyle. No matter how busy we all are, there is one thing we all have in common and that is time. Learning to find ways to write no matter what your schedule is like may be tricky. As I mentioned, I believe in doing small things consistently because eventually it will develop into something.

Here are some practical writing tips that may help you develop your writing.

- Make a habit of writing on a regular basis. Most people are waiting to take the entire day off so they can go write. But I can guarantee you that if you are not already writing a small amount regularly in what little time you have, when your day off comes, you will probably not spend it writing. If you write daily it does not have to be on your book or writing projects. Some days I just write about what is happening in my life just to keep my writing creativity flowing. Most people object to the idea of writing small amounts daily and claim that they are not able to do it like that. If you are not currently producing results and finishing your writing projects then what you are currently doing is not working for you either, so give this a try. You can train and condition yourself.

- Journaling is a good writing habit to have. I mentioned that I have a computer journal that I can password protect and I have several documents that I can cross-reference and search through later. I have one section where I write life events and feelings. Another section is for my accomplishments and answered prayers. In another section I track the dreams I have at night and other writing ideas and comedy. I write snippets, things that strike me funny, or research ideas as they come. Because my journal is on my computer, I can even paste in websites and research on the fly to use in the future. I have a link to the journal I use in the resources area at the end of this book.

- Carry something with you to record your ideas and thoughts as they come throughout the day. Use a pad of paper, digital recorder, or whatever works best for you. I can't count the times I thought I would remember an idea or joke or dream that I had and I would come home later and it would be erased from my mind. I often wonder if our brains can only store so much information and it starts randomly deleting files to make room for more. I carry a pen and grab paper scraps and write things down. Another creative way to remember something later is to call your home voice mail and leave yourself a message. Or use your cell phone to text yourself, take a picture, or record a memo. I recently saw a service available on the Internet where you call a number and leave a voice message which is transcribed into text and then emailed to you.

- I have discovered that I like using a dry erase or whiteboard. I feel so creative when I write on the board. I can sit across the room and see the big picture. I like this so much that I have whiteboards of various sizes everywhere in my house and office. I then use my digital camera to take a picture of the board after I get my thoughts down. I then upload it to my computer and file it. This is my favorite new way of writing sermons. I make a quick outline and draw it on a dry erase board, take a picture and print the picture out and use it as my speaking notes. Works for me!

- I mentioned this before but I think it is worth repeating because it will totally change your writing. When I am writing about a subject that I have a strong opinion about and it is an issue that I would like to see change, I am always careful not to let my anger, strong emotions or hurt come through in my writing. It does not take a genius to point out what is wrong in the world.

It is however very refreshing to hear positive solutions. So what I do is just before I write on a subject I open a second word processing document and start bullet pointing out all the things that are wrong with the subject I am writing on. I call this my "dumping document." I use it as an outlet for all my pet peeves so that when I go to write I am free to be positive. I then try to summarize my rants into one toned-down sentence.

- Find the best time to write based on your lifestyle. Realize this may change based on your current life situation. If you have young children or you are taking a heavy load of classes at school, then you know that writing time may not be easy to find. I used to get up early before anyone else was up and before the telephone started ringing so I could write. Then later as my life got busier I spent the mornings doing office work and the afternoons writing. On a previous writing project, I started writing each night at about 9 PM and stayed at it until the sun came up and then I would sleep until noon. For me it changes with my life situation. Don't think it has to be a certain way. Keep trying things until you find something that works. I switched back to my favorite writing time of getting up at 5 AM and writing until 9.

- Avoid doing administration, mathematics or left-brain thinking just before you write. This took me time to realize about myself. If I get up and start the day by answering a bunch of emails, looking over financial reports or trying to do some type of math or updating my website then I find it harder to write. I either try to do my writing first thing in the morning or minimize my left-brain activity just prior to writing or speaking. On the other hand, if I have been writing for an extended time and I need to switch to administrative tasks I will pull out a calculator or do some math on a piece of paper to get myself back in my left-brain. Sounds unusual but it really does work.

- When the urge strikes, go with it. I am usually working on three to four writing projects at a time. I try to finish at least one major writing project a year. I go back to each project and update it periodically. Occasionally I feel really inspired on a particular subject or project. I found that when this happens, (it is happening to me right now as I write this section on a plane heading to a speaking engagement) stop what you are doing and write for goodness' sake! Don't miss that window of opportunity when creativity knocks. Too often I ignore the urge only to go back later and the inspiration is gone. My wife knows that when my writing inspiration comes it might mean changing my travel plans by getting a hotel and coming home a day later or staying up all night or whatever. You may need to run off to the coffee shop for a few hours or wherever you are free to write. Even as I put the final edits on this book, I awoke this morning at 3:20 a.m. and the urge to write hit me so I got up and have been powering through the last few hours.

- A great way to complete a writing project is to compile a writing team. I find people all the time who would not mind volunteering to help with various aspects of writing. It can be your friends or family, but make sure you can trust them. This is a good way for you to mentor up-and-coming writers. My writing team is informal and fluctuates from time to time. I like to find what a person is good at and plug them in. I have a couple of proofreaders, a few researchers, and people who transcribe audios and do book reports for me. I like to write fast and insert comments in my writing document for others to look up and insert research or quotes later. This allows me to focus on what I do best which is creating the new idea or book. I try not to get sidetracked with research during my writing process. I will make notes to do deeper research later.

- My most recent style of capturing creative thoughts involves writing outlines on my whiteboard, taking a picture and sending it to someone to make an outline. I go back in later and hang the details to the outline. I also send all my sermons, blogs, and articles on a subject to a team member who will put it in a document as a jump-start for me to finish writing later. Get creative, but most important, do not let your process bog you down. If you lose energy for a project, lay it down for a while and switch to something else. Be sure to come back to it later.

What is important about writing is to just do it. When you meet another writer ask them about their process. I love to hear people's stores about how they wrote their first book. You can pick up tips and be encouraged by talking with others who are on the same journey.

## Do I Self-Publish or Use a Publishing Company?

One of the most-asked questions I get about writing is whether it is preferable to self-publish a book or go with a publishing company. First, let me explain the benefits of using the modern technology of e-books and the print on demand services that are readily available. Writing and completing a book is quite challenging, yet it is not the only challenge faced by up-and-coming writers. There are many people who have written a book that was never published. The major reason is that most people have no idea where to get their work published. Not to mention, many fear the loss they might incur in case of lower-than-expected sales. Trends have been changing over time and it is quite difficult to tell which one will work better for you. Below I will discuss some of the possibilities you can explore as a writer if you are interested in writing or publishing a book of your own.

### Books Versus e-Books

As an author many people prefer self-publishing as it gives them all the rights to their book, but in the case of e-books, self-publishing is not the preferred method. With the increased use of the Internet, and portable e-readers such as the Kindle, Nook, and iPad, the popularity of e-books is on the rise. While readers find e-books to be more precise, to-the-point and helpful, writers also find them more affordable and convenient to write. Here are some major advantages of e-books:

- Low cost production,
- All you need is word processor and e-book convertor software such as Adobe Acrobat,

- Low cost of distribution, and
- No hassle of delivering and packaging.

The only drawback of e-books, however, is that this format is not always suitable for all types of books and subjects. People normally won't sit in front of their screen and read 200 page e-books. Not everyone who would benefit from your e-book may own a computer or handheld e-book reading device.

## Consider Printing Your e-Book

Here are a few reasons why you should consider getting your e-book printed. If you are not getting enough online sales despite excellent content, maybe your book is better suited for printed format. If your e-book is a hot seller online, printing it may increase the profit and sales even more offline. It may be wise to use a combination of electronic and printed book formats to reach a variety of people. When it comes to printing e-books, the same old confusion arrives. You can never guarantee that your printed book will sell as much as your e-book. There is good news, though. If you choose to print your e-book, there are inexpensive options such as print-on-demand that allow you to print smaller quantities for reasonable prices.

## Print-On-Demand

*Print-on-demand* (POD) (or *publish* on demand), is a digital printing technology where books or published materials are not printed until an order has been received. POD is now emerging as a very favorable publishing option for aspiring writers. If you want to print your self-published book or e-book, then print-on-demand can greatly minimize the cost in case of disappointing sales. It saves you the cost of printing a large number of copies and keeping stock. With print-on-demand, a book is only published after an order is placed.

Here are just a few of the advantages of print-on-demand:

- Print-on-demand saves you from the worries of return on investments.
- Due to newer technology you can save $5 to $10 per unit printing.
- In some cases, you can order just one book, have it printed and shipped for you.
- As the number of copies printed is limited, the processing time is also less.
- The cost of warehousing and storage is substantially reduced or completely eliminated.

Due to all these reasons, print-on-demand may prove to be extremely profitable from both the individual and business point of view. If you want to get your e-book printed, print-on-demand is by far the best option and even major publishers would be happy to offer you this service. When I published my first book in 2003 I had to print 5,000 copies to get a good discounted price. I can now get the same exact book printed in quantities of 200 for nearly the same price by using POD.

## Using a Publishing Company

Larger publishing companies require more effort to get your book project to print. In order to be accepted, you have to submit a book proposal with a sample chapter. Most book proposals contain a short synopsis of the story, genre, or audience, estimated size, titles, comparative works, etc. You can research the Internet for samples of book proposals. Be sure to check with the publishing company you are planning to approach and see if they have a form or proposal requirements. Like anything else worth pursuing, it is a good idea to find someone else who has already done it and ask them.

Most publishing houses do the following for you:

- Handle all the editing, layout, cover design, and printing of your book.
- File the ISBN and copyright.
- Make your book available to wholesale and retail distribution.
- Do some basic marketing but require you to market too.
- Offer your book on major websites such as Amazon.com.
- Pay you a percent commission on the average price of books they sell.

You are usually required to sign a contract giving them printing rights for an agreed-upon period. Publishing houses normally require the author to purchase a set amount of books at a special author discount. An example of this might be that you are required to buy one thousand or up to three thousand copies or more of your book at a discounted rate. This will allow you to sell your book at events and on your website. You should consider the fact that it will require you to lay out a large amount of money and to maintain a safe, climate-controlled storage of about two pallets of books.

The advantage of using a publishing house is that they help you market your book, cover most of the upfront costs, and file all the legal paper work for you. The downside is that you have to buy and store a large amount of books. Unless you have a great subject and the right timing, you are a seasoned writer, or you already have an audience to market to, don't expect to get rich from your first book. I read somewhere that 95% of all books published sell 5,000 copies or less. I'm not trying to discourage you but I wish someone had told me about this when I published my first book.

Self-publishing is very easy to do now that nearly everything is available over the Internet. The drawback is that you have to do all the marketing yourself. Publishing houses cost more and they help you market, but you still need to do a lot of work if you want to sell your books. Nothing is automatic and you are expected to actively market your book.

Doug Addison

## Copyrights and ISBN

These days, most new and aspiring authors prefer print-on-demand and self-publishing as the most appropriate means of getting their work published. However, getting it published and distributed is not the only thing left to do. Whenever you buy a book, especially from a well-known author and publisher, you will see that besides a very interesting and original cover and front-page, there are many other differences between that book and your self-published book. One of the main differences is the page containing copyright information and the ISBN number.

## Understanding Copyright and ISBN

If you are well aware of the current news regarding the literary world, you must have heard stories regarding people stealing others' work. Even the most popular writers are not safe from plagiarism and redistribution of their work. However, new writers are more likely to be victims of such crimes, as they may not have much proof to provide that their work is original. Copyright is what saves you from such thefts.

An ISBN (International Standard Book Number), on the other hand, is like an electronic identification code for your work including e-books. The ISBN typically is a ten-digit long unique number, which can be deciphered, just like a barcode. Retailers such as bookstores, supermarkets and even libraries use this number to identify your book even if there are many other books of the same title.

## Do You Really Need an ISBN?

Oftentimes, writers and especially e-book authors get really confused about whether they should get copyrights and ISBNs or not. In the case of copyrights, U.S. law defines that you get the copyrights of your work as soon as you finish and file for it. However, there are some significant advantages of getting your copyright actually registered through the U.S. Copyright Office.

If you were considering skipping the copyright and ISBN process, most distributors and retailers won't accept your book. However, if you wish to distribute your e-book online or for free, you can normally do without both.

There are three main reasons for obtaining both.

- Copyrights and an ISBN on your work can give you more credibility as a respected professional author.
- They give you stronger legal support and protection in case of plagiarism and infringements.
- They give you the right to grant usage and publication rights in the event your book goes big.

I personally prefer to get both the copyright and ISBN for all of my published books. You will look much more professional and it makes your book ready for that big break you might get on television or radio.

## How to Obtain Copyrights and ISBN

Every country has different organizations and agencies where authors obtain copyrights and the ISBN. Most well-known publishers and some smaller publishing companies and websites will do this for you at no charge or for a small fee. However, for self-publishing and print-on-demand, you will have to do it on your own.

Obtaining your copyright and ISBN in the United States is fairly simple. You can easily register through the Internet. You will find the application form and a lot of other relevant information on the U.S. Copyright Office site. Depending on the services you register for, the fee can range from $35 to $200.

As for an ISBN, there are numerous agencies that provide this around the world. Here in the U.S., R.R. Bowker is the agency responsible for distributing ISBN numbers. Bowker also has a website where you can apply for an ISBN. The registration fee costs around $25 and you can get a block of ten ISBNs for around $225 at the printing of this book. We have websites listed at the end of this book for you to get applications and pricing.

Copyrighting your material is really easy to do. You can do it all online and save money over filing a paper registration form. For the U.S. you can use the eCO processing section on the Copyright.gov website. You can find the website address at the end of this book in the resource section.

Doug Addison

## How to Market Your Book Using Social Media

"Social media" is defined by Wikipedia as *"media for social interaction, using highly accessible and scalable publishing techniques."* In laymen's terms, social media help people connect online. In popular usage, the term "social media" typically refers to social networking and sharing sites, including the following:

- Blogs
- Forums
- Image/Photo-Sharing Sites
- Video-Sharing Sites
- Twitter
- Facebook
- Linkedin

It has become the battle cry of the new Internet revolution that writers and publishers *must* be involved in social media to succeed online. But with new social media outlets emerging and others going in and out of favor at an ever-increasing pace, it can be hard to keep up. Many frazzled authors are asking themselves and others the following questions: What social media outlets are best for my books? How much time do I need to spend online to be successful? I'm so busy working in my business—how am I going to "tweet," blog, and connect with others online? Do people really care whether or not I'm on Facebook?

Sure, managing your social media efforts can seem frustrating and overwhelming at first glance. As I mentioned previously, you don't have to invest hours and hours posting tweets about what you ate for breakfast, or uploading videos of your cat to YouTube. In fact, you are better off skipping those things.

Instead, approach social media with a plan, and focus on providing and sharing useful information while also interacting with your fans, friends, and followers. If you do that, social media can be an effective and even fun part of your marketing mix. I will be going over the basics of using a few of the most popular social networking sites and strategies. I will also give you some helpful steps you can do in just a few minutes a day.

## Facebook

With over 500 million active users who spend more than 700 billion minutes *per month* online, Facebook is a natural first stop for marketers looking to reach an online audience. The biggest benefits of Facebook include:

- Reach (Nearly everyone is there!)

- Ease of use (If your Dad can figure it out, anyone can)

- Ability to add numerous media, including audio, images, and video to your page

- Ability to email entire groups of fans at a time

If you decide to go the Facebook route, your first step is to create a "Like" page for yourself as an author or publisher. This is basically a profile and expanded bio. Until recently, these pages used to be called "Fan" pages. Personal profiles limit the number of people you can be friends with, while "Like" pages do not. Also, "Like" pages enable you to create an RSS feed and build custom applications. There are a number of tutorials online with step-by-step instructions for creating a "Like" page. Simply do an Internet search on creating a "Like" page on Facebook.

However, if that's overwhelming, I recommend you hire someone to help you with this. You should be able to find someone affordable who can set this up for you. There are lots of people jumping on the Facebook bandwagon who want to make a name for themselves as social media experts.

Once you have created your Facebook "Like" page, here are a few steps to take on a daily basis (I have estimated the time for each to show you that it does not need to take you away from your writing):

- Update your status. Be sure to make it relevant to your audience. Skip the "breakfast" posts unless you're a chef! (one minute)

- Add new blog posts, videos, photos, etc. to your wall. Many other social media sites like Twitter as well as your blog can be set up to add these updates automatically to your wall. (two minutes)

- Review comments on your wall and respond to them. (four minutes)

- Review your news feed and spend a few minutes commenting on posts and updates from your contacts. (four minutes)

- Respond to invitations and messages in your inbox. (two minutes)

- Locate new people to invite to your "Like" page by checking out the friends of current page fans. (two minutes)

This timeframe may seem ambitious, and it is! You may also need a very fast Internet connection to pull it off. Depending on how many messages and posts you actually get, and how quickly you want to add new friends, you might choose to be a bit more flexible.

Still, the idea is to focus on the most important activities and stop when you're done. Sure, you could easily spend the whole day puttering around on Facebook, but your goal is to set a time limit and use it to the max. If you have extra time, you can go back and play Farmville or challenge a friend to a game of Text Twist. Or you could decide to add more friends or get more involved in a conversation. In the meantime, though, get in, get out, and get customers!

## Twitter

Twitter may seem like a relatively new player on the social media front, but the site is actually nearly five years old, having debuted in 2006. Now, Twitter has over 100 million registered users who are sending out a combined 55 million-plus tweets a day. Many people still see Twitter as a waste of time—but didn't they think the same thing about the Internet, 15 or so years ago?

If you're looking for a quick, concise way to reach a wide audience, Twitter may be your answer. Twitter's strength lies in its openness and its numbers. Of course, those are its drawbacks, too. It's so easy to connect with people on Twitter that it isn't much of a commitment—at first, at least.

As an author, you should observe what the "average" user does—and then do the opposite! For instance:

- The average user has fewer than 100 contacts. You will want to aim to increase your reach beyond this.

- The average user's tweet is "chatty." Authors who want to market will want to provide more value.

- The average user hasn't tweeted in the past week. To be successful you will want to stay active.

If you're ready to commit to Twitter, one of the best things you can do is to enlist the help of one of the numerous third-party Twitter applications, such as Hootsuite, Tweetdeck, or Seesmic. These services allow you to track conversations according to numerous keywords, post on different profiles, and create tweets to post at a later time or date. People who are looking for your books will be searching based on keywords. You will want to make a list of some keywords that you know will attract the right people to your books.

Here's what you want to do in about 15 minutes a day:

- Post an update. As with Facebook, make your updates applicable to your audience. Provide a link to your latest blog post or an interesting factoid related to your market. (one minute)

- Check out your new followers. If they look like appropriate contacts (i.e., not spammers), follow them back. (two minutes)

- Respond to DMs, i.e., direct messages, and "@" messages. The latter are tweets aimed directly at you, but posted publicly. (two minutes)

- Check your keywords and hashtags. Through the services suggested above, you can track keywords in your particular niche. Read what people are talking about and asking about; answer questions where you can, and join in conversations where appropriate. (five minutes)

- Read your feed and see what people are talking about. Some of your followers will be chatting about your area of specialty; others won't. Spend a minute or two joining a few conversations, even if it's about who won on *American Idol*. (two minutes)

- Retweet useful information. Did someone tweet a useful tool or a great blog post you think your market will love? Retweet it! You'll generate a positive atmosphere around you while providing great content for your followers. (two minutes)

- Create a few updates to post to Twitter at a later date. Make it look like you're on Twitter more than you are by creating a tweet or two and scheduling it to post later. (one minute)

The key to Twitter success is to be brief and consistent. Users' feeds scroll by so quickly that if you're not in the stream consistently, you're going to fade into the woodwork. Yet if you're out there with useful information frequently, you'll build a loyal following.

**Your Blog**

I wrote about blogging in a previous chapter but now I want to give you some specifics on how to promote your books by utilizing a blog. Many "professional" bloggers would like you to believe that blogging requires a lot of training and fine-tuned skills. That's just not the case. The reality is that if you can hold a conversation with a neighbor or coworker, then you can blog.

The benefits of blogging are many, and have been covered extensively in a variety of other forms. But the bottom line is that blogging is one of the most effective ways to showcase your expertise, connect with potential readers and customers, and establish your on-line persona.

You'll be able to find plenty of books and videos covering the basics of setting up a blog. But what I would like to cover right now is how to blog in 15 minutes a day.

Once your blog is set up, your energy will be spent on two main aspects—adding content and promoting your site. Because both of these topics are critical to the success of your blog, I recommend alternating between them; one day, add a new post or other content to your blog. The next day, spend your 15 minutes promoting your blog. Here's how you can create valuable content:

- Using your book or writing projects, write at least 25 good 300+ word articles (keep them short). Get them ready in advance and update your blog twice a week with them.

- Add a video. Go on YouTube, search for videos in your area of specialty, and pick one to embed in your own blog. Add a few sentences of commentary.

- Record an audio. Hook up your microphone and record a short monologue on your book. Give people some good information. Better yet, use an app on your smartphone and record on the go to save even more time.

- Upload a photo—one of your own, or one you find on a photo-sharing site. Again, make it applicable to your books, and add a few lines of commentary.

- Write a short review of someone else's book or product that adds value to your message.

- Ask someone in your industry a few questions by email and post the interview.

- Answer questions that you receive from readers.

- Create a "round up" of posts or resources online that your readers may be interested in.

Once you've got some great content, the next step is to promote it. On your days off from writing or posting content, use the following to-do list for promoting your blog:

- Link to some of your most popular posts on Facebook, Twitter, or your other social media sites. There are services and plug-ins that will do this for you automatically. (three minutes)

- Respond to comments from readers. You can do this on your blog, in the comments section, or directly by email. (four minutes)

- Create internal links on your blog posts from one link to another. For instance, if you write a post on a great recipe, link to other posts you've written on the same topic. (three minutes)

- Make a few changes to your blog post and submit it to an article posting website. (five minutes)

As with other social media forms, the most important thing to keep in mind is to make your content useful to your audience. You are much better off creating great, useful content twice a week, than throwing up garbage several times a day. Post great stuff, tell people about it, and they will come. If you give useful good quality things away on occasion people will trust you and be more likely to buy your books.

## Other People's Blogs

Commenting on other people's blogs is one of the most overlooked social media strategies, which makes it a great opportunity for you. Not only is there little competition, but it's actually a highly effective way to increase your visibility. By posting on other people's blogs, you'll be able to leverage the other bloggers' success and audience quickly and efficiently.

Before you start posting, though, you need to plan your strategy. Create a list of 10–20 top blogs in the same niche as your books. Choose those that are vibrant and have a strong readership. It won't do you a lot of good to create a passionate, compelling persona on a blog that only a few people are reading, so it's okay to be picky here. You're looking for a site that is a social hub in your industry.

You could approach this task with a variety of goals in mind. For example, you might want to create a relationship with the blogger or with other authors. Your goal might be to establish yourself as an expert. Then again, maybe you just want to create backlinks to give your own blog or website a boost in the eyes of Google. Either way, you'll accomplish your goals by reading posts, making insightful, helpful comments, and building on the conversations already taking place.

Each day, spend fifteen minutes visiting some of the blogs on your list and reading the day's posts. Then make comments where appropriate, and provide links back to your own website or blog. Here are some guidelines to make your efforts most effective:

- Be a gracious guest. First and foremost, keep in mind that you are a guest on someone else's blog. That means you need to be supportive, polite, and kind. You can disagree with what the other blogger has said, but do so in a polite manner. Don't hijack the conversation or steer every post back to you.

- Be thoughtful. No one is going to pay much attention to comments that just say, "Great post! Thanks!" In fact, those kinds of posts are generally considered comment spam and are unlikely to be approved. Instead, respond to the post specifically and provide additional insights or context on the topic. Steer people to places online for additional resources. Sometimes those might be on your blog or website, but sometimes they will be on someone else's site. If you look too self-promotional, don't be surprised if your posts are deleted.

- Stay on track. Imagine this scenario: You and a friend are at Starbucks®, sitting and sipping your lattes, chatting about the best place to buy a digital camera. If someone at the next table suddenly pulled up a chair and said, "I sell ink cartridges—wanna see?" you'd likely roll your eyes and move as far from him as possible. But imagine he said instead, "I'm sorry to interrupt; I overheard what you were saying and I just saw that Joe's Cameras is having a half-off sale on all digital cameras next week. I got mine there and the customer service was awesome!" You'd probably buy the guy a pound of coffee to thank him. See the difference? One comment is about *him*; the other one is about *you*. Keep the comments focused on the conversation already in progress and you'll be a welcome guest.

Commenting on other people's blogs won't make you rich or popular overnight, but it's a great way to build relationships with the movers and shakers—and the customers—in your industry. And those are the types of relationships that last ... and can help you grow your business.

I geared this chapter on Internet and social media marketing specifically towards writers. It will help you increase sales and get your message out to the world once your book published. You can start using these strategies before your book comes out to create a buzz and anticipation. The Internet is an untapped resource sitting right in front of you. I have shown you how you can develop your own social media marketing strategy that you can easily do in a few minutes a day.

Using social media can be overwhelming—but it doesn't have to be. Take a look through all the varieties of sites available, and choose the three or four that best fit your goals, market, and personality. Spending just an hour a day promoting your books online through social networking can have powerful results, but you have to be consistent, both in your image and your efforts. I always say, "Small things done consistently will produce a large amount over time—with a minimal amount of effort."

One last marketing tip: save all your blogs and posts because you can use them later to compile chapters in future books. I know people who convert their blogs to books on a regular basis. Also save some of the feedback and comments that people are posting on your Facebook and your blog. You can use them as endorsements and testimonials on your website.

Doug Addison

## Links and Resources Available to Writers

Some people are naturally gifted to just sit down and write until their project is completed. There are others of us who have a message or destiny from God to write their story or book and need help or guidance in getting started. I wrote this book to be a practical how-to guide on how I learned the hard way. Most of us have the inspiration and creativity to write, but may need encouragement and some practical inside help from others who have written books or are now professional writers.

Most aspiring writers find inspiration and encouragement from those who have been there and done that. There is a lot of help available to those who want guidance but you need to know where to look for it. Sometimes just listening to the stories, experiences, knowledge and passion of people who are living their dream can bring about enough encouragement to wake up and realize your own dream.

Not so long ago, finding such encouragement was not an easy job for new writers. It required a lot of struggle, time and money to hire a writing or literary professional. Today, as the Internet has brought about many moneymaking opportunities for writers, it is also serving as an easily accessible knowledge base and help resource as well. Not only that, you will find that there are an overabundance of websites sharing tips and tricks. You can also find recommendations and reviews for books and journals to read. If you haven't started to look on your own, let me offer you a little boost by sharing some of the most valuable links and resources to get you started.

One of my most used tools when I write is the Google search engine. I no longer spend time looking up facts or quotes, I just Google it and get the response really fast. You can email a webpage to yourself and save it for reference. You can copy and paste quotes right into your writing document then quickly add a footnote of the webpage address in case you need to get permission or as a reference for others.

There are so very many websites available to writers. In listing some website links for writing I am just scratching the surface. Websites are changing all the time. You can check back on my website for updated lists or create your own. Your Internet browser allows you to bookmark a page or add it to your favorites list. I recommend using this feature a lot. Also keep several files on your computer to store articles, webpages, pictures, or things that you like. I am not saying to swipe them but they can help give you ideas and inspiration later.

## General writing resources

www.writing.com is an online community for writers of all genres. It allows the writers to make an online portfolio and share their work. The community also promotes and encourages writing through various contests and competitions.

www.faithwriters.com is a place you can get help and post some of your articles. If you have some e-books, you can begin selling them here. They encourage you to pay for their services but you can use it for article posting like I do.

www.freewritingadvice.com is an excellent website to start with. It has a page for recommended books that a writer must read in order to polish writing skills both in terms of style and creativity.

The http://owl.english.purdue.edu/owl/ is an excellent resource, which offers plenty of help including writing styles and genres. You can also find a list of exercises and movies to help boost your creativity.

http://www.book-publishers-compared.com/ is a database of the most renowned online print on demand and e-book publishers. The site also compares quality and pricing for numerous publishers. You can also find lots of advice and help related to publishing.

While a search engine is the best information resource, http://www.archives.gov/ is a more authentic resource for facts and figures regarding most of the things you might write about in journalism and in fiction.

### Publishing and Print on Demand Websites

www.lulu.com A full service print on demand provider that will also publish your book for you and they offer website hosting options.

www.48hrbooks.com An inexpensive print on demand service for low quantities. They have book layout templates to make it easy.

www.writersedgeservice.com This is a service that helps Christian writers connect with publishers. Check out their Resources page as they have some great links.

www.amazon.com Don't be fooled, authors do not make much money selling on Amazon. They require a very high discount to sell your book. But you really need to be on Amazon if you want to be noticed. Think of the low return as advertising investment. You must list on Amazon!

www.createspace.com This is Amazon's print on demand and self-publishing service. It is actually a good option to consider.

www.isbn.org We mentioned it earlier. You can purchase your own ISBN on this website.

www.copyright.gov/eco/ Copyrighting your material is real easy to do. You can do it all online and save money over filing a paper registration form. For the U.S., use the eCO processing website.

## Great Websites for Online Training and Tutorials

The following are a few websites that offer really good short online video courses on various aspects of writing, blogging, and Internet marketing. You can write a book but unless you get a plan to market it, no one will know about it. The Internet is a great place to do article marketing, video marketing, and social networking.

### The Journal

A good computer-writing journal is hard to find. I have been using The Journal software since 2006. It is a Windows-based program but I run Windows on my Mac just to use The Journal. You can track your writing and cross-reference notes, dreams, or virtually anything. I have developed some training videos to show you how to use it. www.dougaddison.com/thejournal

### WordPress Blog Online Training

If you want to write a book or have one already, you most definitely need a blog. WordPress is the most popular and least expensive blog available. If you want to increase your knowledge of blogging or you are just starting, these simple tutorial videos will take your current blogging experience to the next level. www.BeaBloggerTraining.com

Doug Addison

## Writing Exercises to Help With Creativity

To keep your creative gifts flowing you must use them on a regular basis. Writing is like any other spiritual gift or talent. If you don't use it, you will lose your edge. Even the most renowned writers have suffered from writer's block or a serious slowdown in their creative ideas. Some found a way out and some never picked up a pen again. It was not because of the lack of talent or that they were not creative. It was because they gave up. I want to encourage you to find ways to keep yourself flowing with creativity.

God has given us gifts of creativity. We need to continually use them productively if we want to master our gifts. The best exercise to achieve this is to keep writing. For writers specifically, exercise and practice becomes very essential in order to maximize their strengths and tap into God's creativity. For many years, writers and experts have developed many exercises to stir up creativity. These exercises have proven to be really helpful for both professionals facing a block and new writers looking for an inspiration to start. Let's take a look at some of the tried and tested creativity writing exercises.

## Free-writing

This is the best exercise to get the most amazing new ideas out of your spirit. Set a timer for five to ten minutes and write about anything that comes into your mind. The key is to keep writing without stopping. No corrections, editions or pauses to ponder, even if your writing doesn't make sense. Learn to let things flow out of your spirit. The more you do this, the more it will be like uncapping a river of living water that will flow from you effortlessly.

## Situations and senses

Think of a situation and imagine yourself in it. Write about everything you feel, sense and think when you are there. The best way to do this exercise is to put yourself in any scene of your favorite book or memory and write about it. Your feelings and reactions can be different from the original character or they can be an exaggerated version of the originals. The key is to write whatever comes into your mind without worrying about being too outrageous or too similar to other stories you may have heard. Learn the art of letting it flow from you.

## Object descriptions

Look at an object and write as much of a description about it as you can. Use adjectives, facts and metaphors. You can also create your own objects out of your imagination and make up your own metaphors.

## Object focus

Look at an object and imagine that the object is speaking or communicating a message to you. It does not have to be audible words. Now write about what it is saying.

## Make up a character chart

Try to think or make up a character. Focus on every single detail starting from appearance to personality traits. Make up a chart of all the attributes ranging from the color of his/her hair to things he/she hates and loves, from profession to hobbies and daily routines.

## Views on news

Take a story out of a newspaper and write your own views on it. Write about its future impact, background and any personal story you can relate to it. You can also pick a very old newspaper and write about its consequences and reviews.

## Group exercise

Now, this is one the most fun and enjoyable one. The more players you can get to play with, the more fun it will be. Ask each one of the players to start a random story. Set the timer for two to three minutes. After the time is up, put everyone's paper in a hat and shuffle. Tell everyone to make a random pick and continue the story written on it. Edits and corrections are not permitted.

## Things I did when I was a kid

Write about things that you used to like to do as a child. What was it that you wanted to do when you grew up? Who or what did you want to become?

## If money were no object I would

Write 300 words, 500 words, and 1200 words on this theme. This exercise gives you a chance to start small and grow your article as you add richer details.

## 1000, 800, 500, 300

Write a 1500-word document about your favorite topic. Now rewrite it in 1000 words. From there, edit its length to 800 words. Now try summarizing it further to 500 words, and finally, in as succinct a version as you can muster. Create the document one last time in no more than 300 words without losing its meaning.

## Closing Word of Encouragement

When it comes to writing it is best to just do it! Don't wait for the perfect opportunity or for things to line up for you or the right amount of free time because in reality the right circumstances seldom happen. Just start now by opening a word processing document and write down a few ideas about your book. You can start with whom it is going to be written to (target audience) and a few paragraphs about what you want to communicate. Next skip a few lines down the page and start creating some bullet points of ideas for the book. Don't worry about the title or getting everything perfect. Just get a page or two of ideas and outlines. Now go back later and add more and over time it will start to fill up.

If you need help getting motivated, I wrote a book that has helped many people get started. *Personal Development God's Way* has exercises that will teach you how to take small steps consistently over time toward what you feel destined to do. I started writing this small book over three years ago. I went back and added to it again and again until I got it to a place of editing and self-publishing. On the other hand, I wrote *Spiritual Identity Theft Exposed* in a matter of weeks. It just flowed out of me very quickly and I used some of my previous blogs to give it more substance.

We are all creative and we all have a story that can help someone else. Books, e-books, websites, blogs, and articles are great tools of communicating. Even writing text messages and emails can be a good way to start.

Writing is an art and there are a lot of resources out there to help you get your artistic creation into the hands of the people that would benefit most. You were uniquely created by God and there is no one else who can do the things that you do in the way that you do them. If you have a feeling inside that you are supposed to write a particular book then you are in good company. People everywhere are sharing their stories and creations all the time.

Let me know if this small book has helped you in any way. You can tell me by going to my website www.dougaddison.com or to one of my social networking pages that are listed on my website. May God rich bless everything you place your pen to!

I wish you all the best.

Doug Addison

## *Other Resources from Doug Addison*

**Personal Development God's Way**
272 pages 2010
People everywhere want to know their life purpose and destiny. God's desire for us all is nothing but the best. *Personal Development God's Way* was developed after Doug Addison spent a lifetime of studying why some people's lives change radically and others do not. This book is full of practical examples, stories, and detailed study questions designed to apply what you learn to your life.

**Accelerating Into Your Life's Purpose**
**10 Audio CDs & 62 page Journal 2007**
Discover your destiny, awaken passion, and transform your life with this 10 day interactive program. Designed to reveal your life's desires, remove obstacles, and create a written plan for what to focus on next.

**Spiritual Identity Theft Exposed**
**67 pages 2011**
The rise of identity theft in the world today parallels what is happening spiritually to people all around the world. People have been blinded to their true identity and the destiny they were created to live. Contains seven strategies to

*For more information visit*
*www.dougaddison.com or call (800) 507-7853*